O9-CFT-207

RACHEL CARSON

The Wonder of Nature

RACHEL CARSON

The Wonder of Nature

Catherine Reef
Illustrated by Larry Raymond

Twenty-First Century Books

A Division of Henry Holt and Co., Inc.

Frederick, Maryland

Published by
Twenty-First Century Books
A Division of Henry Holt and Co., Inc.
38 South Market Street
Frederick, Maryland 21701

Text Copyright © 1992
Catherine Reef

Illustrations Copyright © 1992
Twenty-First Century Books

Printed in the United States of America

10 9 8 7 6 5 4 3 2 1

Library of Congress Cataloging in Publication Data

Reef, Catherine
Rachel Carson: The Wonder of Nature
Illustrated by Larry Raymond

(An Earth Keepers Book)
Includes glossary and index.
Summary: Follows the life of the biologist and conservationist,
known for her writing on the environment.
1. Carson, Rachel, 1907-1964—Juvenile literature.
2. Ecologists—United States—Biography—Juvenile literature.
3. Conservationists—United States—Biography—Juvenile literature.
[1. Carson, Rachel, 1907-1964. 2. Conservationists. 3. Biologists.]
I. Raymond, Larry, ill. II. Title.
III. Series: Earth Keepers
QH31.C33R44   1991
574'.092—dc20 [B] 91-19778 CIP AC
ISBN 0-941477-38-X

93-680

Contents

"Most of us walk unseeing
through the world."

Chapter 1

A World Unseen

It was a summer night in 1959. It was a hot night for a community meeting, but the men and women of Silver Spring, Maryland, needed to make an important decision. They were about to vote on whether or not to spray their neighborhood with a pesticide, a strong chemical that kills insect pests.

Some people hoped that spraying would get rid of the bothersome insects, such as mosquitoes and gnats, that can make the Maryland summer so unpleasant. But not everyone favored using pesticides to control these insects. Some people worried about the harmful effects that spraying might have. Were these chemicals safe to use? Could they hurt more than unwanted insects?

Other people were ready to go ahead with the spraying. They didn't believe that pesticides could be dangerous for people to use.

One of the people present at the meeting, however, knew just how harmful pesticides can be. Rachel Carson waited patiently for her turn to speak.

The woman with gentle brown curls and friendly eyes was normally soft-spoken and shy. But on this night, Rachel Carson spoke out strongly. Pesticides *do* destroy more than unwanted insects, she said. They are poisons that threaten other forms of life as well.

When sprayed on bushes and trees, she said, pesticides kill songbirds, honeybees, and other welcome creatures. What could such spraying do to the children who play near the sprayed areas and breathe the poisoned air?

Pesticides also harm animals that are not sprayed by these poisons. Carson explained that pesticide spraying starts a chain of poisoning that hurts all forms of life. For example, pesticides can land on plankton, the tiny animals and plants that float on lakes and ponds. This plankton, Carson observed, is food for water fleas and other tiny insects. Fish depend on these insects for their food. But when fish eat poisoned insects, they swallow the chemical poisons, too. Because one fish can eat many insects, its body is likely to contain a high level of pesticides.

The chain of poisoned food does not stop there, Rachel Carson continued. Animals that eat poisoned fish, or other food that has been sprayed, swallow these pesticides, too. The chemical poisons then find their way into the animals' bodies, where they may remain for life. At each step in the food chain, the level of pesticides in the animals' bodies grows higher.

People, too, are part of the food chain, Carson told her audience. And people consume pesticides when they eat poisoned fish or other animals. Pesticides also enter people's bodies when they eat fruit and vegetables that farmers have sprayed with these chemicals.

A person may get only a small amount of pesticides with each serving of fish or vegetables or fruit. But these poisons remain and build up in the body. If the level of pesticides in the body grows high enough, Carson argued, these chemicals could be a danger to a person's health. Pesticides might cause serious illnesses such as cancer, a disease that attacks and destroys the body's healthy cells and tissues.

The people who listened on that hot, muggy night knew Rachel Carson as a scientist and the author of best-selling books about the sea. They did not know that her next book, *Silent Spring*, would warn the world about the dangers of pesticides. Rachel Carson spoke for only 15 minutes. But because of the facts that she presented, the group voted not to spray.

Although Carson spoke about pesticide spraying that summer night, she really was speaking about a much larger subject—the way living things are linked to each other and their environment. Living things are connected to each other in a natural network of relationships called an ecosystem. Each plant or animal species depends on the other living things in that ecosystem for its survival. However, as Rachel Carson pointed out, the natural network of living things can easily be hurt—it can even be permanently destroyed.

Today, many people are worried about the environment. Governments, businesses, and citizen groups are working to keep our natural surroundings clean and safe. This work includes stopping the sources of pollution. It involves conservation, or preserving our natural resources, and setting aside land for parks and wilderness areas. It means saving endangered plant and animal species from becoming extinct.

However, until Rachel Carson wrote *Silent Spring*, the relationship between living things and their environment was not understood very well. People thought that they could use chemicals freely to control their environment. They commonly kept pesticides in their homes and used these chemical sprays to kill any insect that happened to wander indoors. They used pesticides in their yards and gardens. Few people knew that by spraying mosquitoes, beetles, or flies, they risked harming other wildlife—and themselves as well.

In other words, most people did not understand how living creatures depend on each other in a network of relationships. People did not understand that what one living thing does can affect many other living things, or that by changing one part of an ecosystem, we risk changing other parts of the network.

Rachel Carson was one of America's first ecologists, a person who studies living things in their environment. Her studies of the ocean world show the relationships between soaring ocean birds and rock-bound mollusks, between animal and plant life, between small fish and large ones, and even between life in the sea and human life on land.

Carson devoted her life and work to describing these natural relationships. She described how fragile, or easily destroyed, these relationships are. She taught her fellow human beings that protecting the environment is something everyone needs to do.

"Most of us walk unseeing through the world," Rachel Carson wrote in *Silent Spring*. Many people fail to notice nature's beauty, she stated. They know little about the plants and animals that live around them. They know even less about their place in this world of living things.

It took Rachel Carson's scientific knowledge, writing talent, and respect for the wonder of nature to show people that they, too, are a part of the unseen world.

Chapter 2

A Child's World

Rachel Louise Carson was born on May 27, 1907, in Springdale, Pennsylvania, a country spot about 18 miles from Pittsburgh. At that time, it was a rugged place for a child to grow up.

The Carsons' tiny wooden house had no electricity, heat, or plumbing. The family prepared their meals in a lean-to kitchen attached to the house. Their bathroom was the nearby outhouse. The Carsons picked and sold apples, pumped water from a well, and made their own butter and cheese.

They kept a variety of animals. Young Rachel watched chicks peck their way through eggshells and cows graze in the meadow. She held rabbits in her lap and cupped kittens carefully in her hands. The Carsons' land, bordering the Allegheny River, contained many acres of woods. So Rachel got to know the wild plants and animals as well. With her dog, Candy, she recalled, Rachel spent "a great deal of time in the woods and beside streams, learning the birds and the insects and the flowers."

The Carson family was a loving and close-knit one. They often enjoyed evenings together around the piano in the living room. Still, years later, Rachel would recall that she was "a solitary child." With no neighbors living nearby, she did not often play with other children. Her sister and brother, Marian and Robert, Jr., were teen-agers. They loved their little sister but had interests of their own.

Supporting the family kept Rachel's father busy much of the time. For a while, Robert Carson, Sr., tried to make money by selling pieces of his land. But that plan was not very successful. So Rachel's father sold insurance and worked in a power plant.

Rachel's best friend and companion was her mother, Maria. Maria Carson had been a teacher before she was married. She had enjoyed teaching and sometimes missed it, although Maria was often a teacher to her youngest child, Rachel.

Maria Carson taught Rachel at home on the many days when the girl was absent from school. The cautious mother would not take any chances with Rachel's health. She kept her daughter home from school whenever she worried that Rachel might catch a cold. Rachel did well in her home school, though, and easily kept up with her class.

Maria Carson's love of nature provided Rachel with valuable lessons. Maria showed her curious daughter the surprising creatures hiding under rocks, nesting in trees, and resting in stream-side grasses. But her mother taught Rachel more than the names and homes of wild animals. She shared with her daughter, as Rachel later wrote, "her deep love of nature and of all living things."

"A child's world is fresh and new and beautiful, full of wonder and excitement," Rachel wrote years later. But she knew that, far too often, children lose their delight in the world as they grow up.

For a child to keep alive "the inborn sense of wonder," Rachel Carson wrote, he or she "needs the companionship of at least one adult who can share it." Together, they can discover "the joy, excitement, and mystery of the world we live in."

To a large extent, it was Maria Carson who nourished and kept alive Rachel's sense of wonder. Thanks to her mother's thoughtful teaching, Rachel grew up close to the earth and its creatures. "I can remember no time when I wasn't interested in the out-of-doors and the whole world of nature," Rachel recalled as an adult.

The world of nature wasn't just something that Rachel enjoyed outdoors—she read about it in books as well. At first, she enjoyed stories with animals for characters, such as *The Tale of Peter Rabbit*. Yet as she grew older, Peter's antics in Mr. McGregor's garden lost their appeal. Stories in which rabbits and squirrels acted like people showed a false picture of the natural world. Instead, Rachel chose to read about animals as they really lived in the wild.

Another part of nature captured Rachel's interest, too. Growing up in the rugged countryside of Pennsylvania, Rachel often dreamed of the vast, far-off ocean, which she had never seen. "I dreamed of it, and I longed to see it, and I read all the sea literature I could find," she said.

Rachel also enjoyed reading *St. Nicholas*, a children's magazine that printed stories and poems by its readers. When she was 10 years old, Rachel sent a story of her own to *St. Nicholas*. Her story told about pilots in World War I, a war the United States had entered in 1917.

Rachel closely followed the news about the fighting in Europe, where soldiers from the United States fought the German army. She had a personal reason to be very concerned. Her brother, Robert, had recently joined the U.S. Army Aviation Service.

Rachel's story was called "A Battle in the Clouds." It told of a Canadian pilot whose airplane was damaged in a battle over Europe. With his plane about to fall from the sky, the brave pilot "crawled out along the wing, inch by inch, until he reached the end. He then hung from the end of the wing, his weight making the plane balance properly." The German soldiers admired the pilot's skill and courage so much that they let him land safely.

It was an unusual story for one written during World War I. At that time, because of the war, many people across the United States disliked Germans. But Rachel's story showed that she knew, even at an early age, that people should not be judged by their nationality or race. "A Battle in the Clouds" demonstrated Rachel's belief that a person's own qualities are what really matter.

The editors of *St. Nicholas* liked Rachel's story so much that they not only printed it, they awarded her the Silver Badge, or second prize. For the rest of her life, Rachel Carson remembered her excitement at hearing the good news. "Perhaps that early experience of seeing my work in print," Rachel recalled years later, "played its part in fostering my childhood dream of becoming a writer."

This early accomplishment encouraged Rachel to do more than just dream about being a writer. She wrote more stories and submitted them to *St. Nicholas*. In one, a group of French soldiers expressed their joy upon learning that the United States had entered World War I. For this story, Rachel received the Gold Badge—first prize!

Chapter 3

To the Sea

Throughout her school years, Rachel Carson remained interested in being an author. In high school, she worked hard and received good grades on the compositions that she wrote. Hoping to go to college, Rachel was a serious student, with little time to spend with friends. Still, her classmates liked Rachel's quiet cheerfulness. Some of them wrote a friendly rhyme about Rachel that appeared in the high-school yearbook:

> *"Rachel's like the mid-day sun*
> *Always very bright*
> *Never stops her studying*
> *'Til she gets it right."*

Rachel was rewarded for her hard work and good grades. In 1925, she was admitted to the Pennsylvania College for Women (now called Chatham College). There, she chose English literature as her major, the main subject that she would study.

From her earliest years, Rachel thought that "it would be fun to make up stories." Now, as a young woman, she was eager to become a good writer, to make up stories and poems that people would like to read. She knew that, in order to master the art of writing, she must read and study the work of other writers.

Rachel quickly put her writing skills to use. In her first year at college, Rachel was a reporter for the school newspaper. She also wrote stories for a school magazine and worked on the college yearbook. In her second year, one of Rachel's stories won the prize for best composition.

But her life at college was not all work. Rachel enjoyed playing sports and often joined the other young women for games of softball, field hockey, and basketball. Sometimes she would invite a college friend home to spend a weekend with her family.

At school, Rachel kept another one of her interests from her earliest years: her love of nature. In one of her college compositions, she described herself as "intensely fond" of the outdoors. "I am never happier," she wrote, "than when I am before a glowing campfire with the open sky above my head. I love all the beautiful things of nature and the wild creatures are my friends."

In the spring of her second year at college, Rachel's interest in "all the beautiful things of nature" led her to make a decision that surprised her teachers—and herself. A class in biology, the study of living things, changed the course of Rachel Carson's life.

Professor Mary Skinker taught Rachel's first biology course. Full of energy and enthusiasm, Mary Skinker was as fascinated by the mystery and order of nature as her student was. Professor Skinker urged Rachel to continue her studies in science.

As the class explored woodlands for traces of animal life and looked at living cells under microscopes, Rachel felt that this was how she wanted to spend her life. She decided to become a scientist, not a writer. Rachel changed her major subject of study to biology.

Rachel's other professors warned her that this was a mistake. There were very few jobs for women scientists in the 1920s. She would be lucky even to find a position teaching biology, they argued. And what a waste of her writing talent!

Rachel was determined to be a scientist, but that did not mean she let her writing talent go to waste. She still wrote poems, and she still loved to read. On one rainy night, she read the poem "Locksley Hall," by Alfred, Lord Tennyson. As the storm beat against the windows of her room, Rachel came to the powerful last line of the poem: "And the mighty wind arises, roaring seaward, and I go."

Although she had never seen the ocean, those words caused Rachel, once again, to feel drawn by the power and mystery of the sea. She later recalled how the poem "burned itself in my mind." As the sea seemed to call to a character in the poem, so it called to Rachel. She said that the poem "spoke to something within me, seeming to tell me that my own path led to the sea."

Rachel graduated with honors from the Pennsylvania College for Women in 1929. With her good grades and help from Mary Skinker, she earned a scholarship to study at The Johns Hopkins University in Baltimore, Maryland. Rachel planned to take courses in marine zoology, the study of the animals of the sea.

Before school started in the fall, Rachel had a chance to spend a few weeks at the Marine Biological Laboratory in Woods Hole, Massachusetts. Every summer, biologists from many colleges and universities traveled to Cape Cod, a sandy peninsula on the Atlantic coast, to study marine life at the Woods Hole laboratory.

There, Rachel finally saw with her own eyes the sea that she had read so much about. She watched waves break against the shore and spotted strange sea creatures, such as the Portuguese man-of-war, floating by with the ocean's currents.

Surrounded by the vast ocean, Rachel and the other students at Woods Hole helped the scientists with their many research projects. Rachel followed the swimming patterns of mackerel at sea, cut open oysters to study their organs, and peered through a microscope at tiny sea plants and animals.

Rachel Carson was now 22 years old. She had seen the ocean at last. And she knew that her decision to study science was the right one for her.

Filled with excitement, Carson began her studies in Baltimore that fall. But her summer freckles had barely started to fade when an event occurred that changed the lives of all Americans.

In October 1929, the U.S. economy collapsed. This time in America's history is known as the Great Depression. Banks closed, and many families lost their life savings. Factories shut down, and many men and women lost their jobs. Across the United States, tens of thousands of people were out of work and penniless. Unemployed men and women searched anxiously for any work they could find, and needy people waited in long lines for soup and bread.

During these hard times, the Carson family banded together to save money. Robert and Maria Carson left their farm and moved in with Rachel. Robert, Jr., joined the household briefly in 1933, working now and then as a radio repairman. Rachel's sister, Marian, now divorced, and Marian's two daughters lived with the family for a while, too.

It was hard for a woman to find work as a scientist before, but the weak economy made it almost impossible. Now there were fewer jobs available for men as well as women. After she finished her studies in 1932, Carson felt lucky to get part-time work teaching at Johns Hopkins and the University of Maryland. To earn extra money, she wrote articles about marine life for a Baltimore newspaper.

But when her father died suddenly in 1936, Carson had to support her mother and herself. Concerned about this new responsibility, Carson tried harder to find better paying work. Her search took her to the U.S. Bureau of Fisheries in Washington, D.C.

The Bureau of Fisheries put on a radio show called "Romance Under the Waters." In the 1930s, many families gathered together at night to listen to the radio. In the days before television, people often depended on the radio for entertainment, news, and educational programs. The short radio broadcasts produced by the Bureau of Fisheries provided people with interesting facts about sea life.

The day Carson entered the bureau for an interview, she found that the chief of the biology division, Elmer Higgins, had a difficult problem. Higgins could not find someone to write the radio scripts. He had hired a radio writer, but that person did not know enough about marine biology. He had tried the biologists on his staff, but they could not seem to produce entertaining scripts. Pleased to see Carson in his office, Elmer Higgins decided to try again. He gave Carson a chance to write the scripts.

It was a turning point in Rachel Carson's life.

Carson hurried home and wrote the best script that she could. Higgins liked her work and offered her a part-time job. At last, Carson realized that she didn't have to decide between being either a scientist or a writer. She could combine the two careers. "It dawned on me that by becoming a biologist I had given myself something to write about," she said.

Maria and Rachel Carson moved to a small house in Silver Spring, Maryland, to be close to Washington, D.C. When Marian died later that year, Rachel's two nieces, Marjorie and Virginia, came to live with them. Now Rachel found herself with a family of four to support.

Eager to earn more money, Carson took a civil service test, the examination given for government jobs. If she received a high grade on the test, she could become a full-time marine biologist with the federal government. Carson was the only woman to take the test—and the person who received the highest grade. The Bureau of Fisheries hired her as a full-time junior biologist.

Carson enjoyed her work. In a small office, she wrote her short radio scripts. "Seven-Minute Fish Tales," her co-workers called them. But that was only part of her job. Carson also answered the many questions that the bureau received from people across the country.

She was especially pleased when Elmer Higgins gave her a new assignment. He asked her to write something about the sea—something longer than the seven-minute radio scripts she was used to writing.

Carson's imagination went to work. "Who has known the ocean?" she began. She went on to describe the strange sights and sensations of the sea world, a mysterious and unfamiliar place to most people. There, waves beat over crabs hiding near the shore, and sunlight became a bluish glow 100 feet below the surface.

Higgins read Carson's work and handed it back to her. Behind his small, round glasses, the division chief's eyes twinkled. Carson had done a good job—too good, in fact, for the Bureau of Fisheries, he said. Higgins was so impressed with her writing that he urged Carson to send this piece to the *Atlantic Monthly*, one of the country's best magazines. Perhaps, Higgins suggested to Carson, her piece would be published there.

It took Carson weeks to work up her nerve to send the piece out. And it took another six weeks to receive a response. But she would never forget the moment when she heard that her piece was going to be published.

Carson had written her first professional article. From that point on, she said, "everything else followed."

Chapter 4

Wind, Sea, and Birds

Today, it is common to see films and programs about ocean life. But in the days before television, few people ever saw the strange and fascinating underwater world that Rachel Carson described.

When her article first appeared in the *Atlantic Monthly*, many readers were amazed to discover that the ocean is such a busy place, alive with interesting creatures. It is the home, Carson wrote, "of the hundred-foot blue whale, the largest animal that ever lived. It is also the home of living things so small that your two hands might scoop up as many of them as there are stars in the Milky Way."

Editors at Simon and Schuster, a book publisher, were certain that people would be eager to read more about sea life. They asked Carson to write a book—a book that would make the sea as real and beautiful to readers as it was to her.

Carson gladly began this project, although it meant three years of very hard work. Her job at the Bureau of Fisheries kept her busy during the day, so she wrote the book, titled *Under the Sea-Wind*, on weekends and late at night. Often her cats, Buzzie and Kito, were Carson's only company. They took turns lying on the finished pages piled next to her typewriter.

It was hard, tiring work, but Carson's belief that "the life of the sea is worth knowing" kept her from quitting.

In *Under the Sea-Wind*, Carson wrote about life on the shore, in the open waters of the sea, and on the ocean floor. She told of sea birds "huddled close together, wing to wing," trying to survive a winter storm. She showed her readers the newly hatched mackerel, "no larger than a poppy seed, drifting in the surface layers of pale green water." Her words painted a picture of silver eels traveling on their "far sea journey."

Carson also explained the concept of ecology, how one species depends on others for survival. The ocean world is a network of living things, she explained. Human beings have a place in the life of the sea, too.

Carson's book described a group of fishermen who depended on the sea for their livelihood. She told of one young fisherman in particular. "Only two years at sea," he had not yet lost his sense of wonder about the world below. Though he made a living catching fish, he admired the beauty and strength of the creatures in his net.

One time, this young fisherman leaned over the side of his boat to see "the race and rush and downward whirl of thousands of mackerel. He suddenly wished he could be down there, a hundred feet down, on the lead line of the net. What a splendid sight to see those fish streaking by at top speed in a blaze of meteoric flashes!"

Scientists praised *Under the Sea-Wind* when it was published in 1941, but the public ignored Carson's book. At that time, world events, not the busy life of the sea, were foremost on people's minds. Armies were once again on the march, across Europe and Asia. Then, on December 7, Japanese planes attacked the U.S. naval base at Pearl Harbor, Hawaii. In a radio broadcast, President Franklin D. Roosevelt told the shocked American people that the United States had entered World War II.

For the next four years, Americans battled overseas, mostly in Europe and on small islands in the South Pacific. U.S. Navy ships carried troops and equipment to faraway shores. Fighter planes took off from the decks of huge aircraft carriers, and submarines patrolled the depths of the ocean.

To guide those ships safely, the Navy needed to have the most accurate information about the oceans. Scientists made new studies of the seas. They tracked the course of the ocean currents, they measured how deep the seas were, and they mapped the features of the ocean floor. At work, Carson read about the discoveries in this new branch of science called oceanography.

During and after World War II, Carson took on more tasks at work and met them with energy and commitment.

In 1949, she became editor-in-chief. She was now in charge of the entire publishing program of the Bureau of Fisheries (renamed the Fish and Wildlife Service).

As part of that program, Carson wrote a series of booklets called "Conservation in Action," describing wildlife refuges. In these protected areas, animals lived freely in their natural habitats. To gather information for the series, Carson visited refuges from Oregon to New Hampshire. She enjoyed seeing animals in the wild and wrote vivid descriptions of them for her readers. "I'd like to spend all my time doing just that sort of thing," she said.

Most of the time, though, her job kept Carson seated at her desk. Her office was bigger now, but she had less and less time to do the kind of work she really loved— exploring and writing about nature, especially her favorite subject, the sea. She wanted to start another book, one that included the exciting, new studies in oceanography. "In the mood for a change of some sort," Carson looked for a job that would give her more time to write.

When she had no success finding a position, Carson decided that she would have to make time—at nights and on weekends—to work on her new project. This book, called *The Sea Around Us*, would give readers a complete portrait of the sea, in all of its wonder and beauty.

Once again, Carson got busy. She often traveled home from work with a carload of library books and scientific journals. She read more than a thousand research studies and wrote letters to scientists around the world. Carson collected information on every aspect of ocean life. "Just plain hard slogging," she called this work.

Carson had really begun this research years earlier. "In a sense," she wrote, "I have been collecting material on this ocean book all my life—ever since childhood I've been fascinated by the sea. And my mind has stored up everything I have ever learned about it as well as my own thoughts, impressions, and emotions."

As hard-working as she was, Carson made time for some fun. She and her family began to spend summers in Maine, on the banks of the Sheepscot River. They rented a cabin so close to the ocean ("on the very edge of the water," Rachel Carson wrote) that they could hear the soothing roar of the surf.

Sometimes Carson took field trips with her friend and co-worker, Shirley Briggs. Briggs shared Carson's love of nature and the outdoors. One autumn, Carson and Briggs traveled to Hawk Mountain Sanctuary in Pennsylvania to watch the migrating hawks. To Carson, they looked "like brown leaves drifting on the wind."

Even when Carson sat on a mountain looking up at the sky, her thoughts were never far from the sea. Settled against the cold rocks of Hawk Mountain, she realized that she was "at the bottom of another ocean—an ocean of air on which the hawks are sailing."

Carson had a different adventure in 1949, after she consulted Dr. William Beebe about her new book. Beebe was famous for exploring the ocean in a round diving chamber called a bathysphere. Knowing Carson's plans for a new book, he told her, "You can't write this book until you have gotten your head under water."

Carson followed Beebe's advice in Florida that July. Wearing weights on her feet to hold her down, Carson locked herself in a clumsy diving suit with a large metal helmet. She dove into the water, breathing air pumped through a tube connected to the ship above her.

The helmet's crude mask looked like a thick, barred window, but that didn't stop Carson from noticing the beautiful underwater sights. "I learned what the surface of the water looks like from underneath," she wrote. She saw "how exquisitely delicate and varied are the colors displayed by the animals on the reef. I got the feeling of the misty green vistas of a strange, nonhuman world."

Carson remembered those scenes while she wrote *The Sea Around Us*. Her words created bold and lively pictures, a portrait of an underwater world so lifelike that a person reading the book could almost see the mysterious sea creatures or feel the strong ocean tides that Carson described. People enjoyed these descriptions so much that when it was published in 1950, *The Sea Around Us* quickly became a best seller. It won both scientific and literary awards and was translated into 32 languages. Soon Carson's eager readers also began to buy her first book, *Under the Sea-Wind*, and in 1952 it became a best seller, too.

At last, Rachel Carson had found the "something" that would allow her to spend as much time as she wanted by the shore or at her typewriter. She now earned enough money from her books to quit her job. Carson fulfilled another dream, too. She bought land on the coast of Maine and built a summer home.

In Maine, Carson spent many mornings wading into tidepools and gathering different types of sea life. "I can't think of any more exciting place," she said. Carson could easily spend hours exploring the living world of the Maine seacoast. Once, the icy water made her body so numb that she had to be carried to shore!

Those days by the sea helped Carson to write her next book, *The Edge of the Sea*, which described the Atlantic coastline from Maine to Florida. To Carson, the shore was "a world apart," a special place where "the only sounds were those of the wind and the sea and the birds."

Carson loved to share this world with her family. She introduced her niece Marjorie's son, Roger, to the wonder of the sea when he was just a baby. In the years ahead, Rachel and Roger would spend long summer days by the shore—wandering along the coast, scampering over rocks, or wading through tidepools.

At night, Rachel and Roger would walk on the beach with a flashlight to catch a glimpse of ghost crabs. These tiny, gray creatures bury themselves in the sand during the day, but scurry silently over the beach at night.

A walk in the Maine woods with Roger, Rachel said, was a journey of "exciting discovery." Roger and Rachel—they were "two friends," she observed—would share new "adventures in the world of nature."

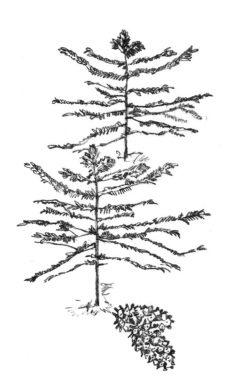

This sharing, Carson wrote, "includes nature in storm as well as calm, by night as well as day, and is based on having fun together rather than on teaching." These two friends would enjoy a rainy-day walk in the fog of the Maine woods. They would pretend that the young spruce seedlings (trees as little as Roger's finger) were Christmas trees for squirrels.

Rachel Carson wrote about her adventures with Roger for a magazine called the *Woman's Home Companion*. Later, that article became a book, *The Sense of Wonder*. In this work, Carson advised parents to help their children enjoy the wonders of nature. Parents did not need to give their children a great deal of information, she wrote. It was enough to share with them a love of nature's beauty.

For both children and their parents, Rachel Carson said, "it is not half so important to *know* as to *feel*." She wanted children to gain a feeling for the wonder of nature rather than simply learn scientific names and facts.

In the beauty of the earth, Carson wrote, parents and children would find "strength that would endure as long as life lasts."

Chapter 5

A Silent Spring

In 1957, Carson received a troubling letter from her friend Olga Owens Huckins, a writer and bird lover in Duxbury, Massachusetts. Rachel Carson had known Olga Huckins and her husband for years. They had created a sanctuary, or protected area, for birds, and Carson knew that they cared about nature as much as she did.

Mrs. Huckins had a problem. Recently, workers from the state government had sprayed local salt marshes with DDT (dichloro-diphenyl-trichloroethane), a pesticide. The government had hoped to destroy the mosquitoes that bred in the salt marshes, but the wind had carried the DDT to the Huckins's beloved bird sanctuary.

Once the pesticide had reached the sanctuary, it killed grasshoppers, bees, and many birds. "All of these birds died horribly, and in the same way," Mrs. Huckins wrote.

"Their bills were gaping open, and their splayed claws were drawn up to their breasts in agony."

But now the mosquitoes were as bad as ever, Mrs. Huckins reported, and the government planned to spray again. She asked for Carson's help in getting scientists to call for a ban on this type of spraying, which she felt was neither needed nor wanted.

Rachel Carson had been concerned about the use of pesticides before she read Mrs. Huckins's letter. People across the United States were spraying these chemicals on lawns and woodlands to kill mosquitoes and other insect pests. Pesticides such as DDT were also commonly used on the crops that farmers grew each year.

Many government, industry, and scientific authorities praised these chemicals as a great benefit to people. They claimed that chemical pesticides were perfectly safe. But other scientists and concerned citizens, including Carson, were not so sure. They thought that researchers had to learn more about the effects of these pesticides.

Upset by her friend's letter, Carson read more about pesticides, and she soon discovered some worrisome facts. Again and again, Carson read reports of wildlife being killed and people being poisoned. She also learned that pesticides killed many insects that served as natural pest controls. Without these natural insect controls, harmful or bothersome insects actually grew in number. "The more I learned about the use of pesticides," Carson wrote, "the more appalled I became."

Struck by the evidence before her, Carson realized that she needed to do more than alert scientists to the problem. She needed to write a book for the general public.

Rachel Carson had spent a lifetime informing people about the wonder of nature. Now she had to inform them about the danger of pesticide use. "What I discovered," she recalled, "was that everything which meant the most to me as a naturalist was being threatened, and that nothing I could do would be more important."

It was a hard time for Carson to begin such a project. Her family kept her busier than ever. Her niece Marjorie recently had died. Marjorie had been a widow, and now Marjorie's son, five-year-old Roger, was an orphan. As a loving aunt, Carson adopted the boy and became a mother for the first time.

When she wasn't packing picnic baskets and taking Roger to the beach, Carson had to care for her mother. Maria Carson was almost 90 years old and not in good health. Rachel, now 50 years old, was not well either. She suffered from arthritis (a painful swelling of the body's joints), sinus trouble, and a stomach ulcer—"a catalog of illnesses," she called them.

But Carson thought about the many flocks of birds she had watched fly overhead, and how she had admired their beauty. She remembered the tiny creatures that she had fished from the shore for study, and then lovingly returned to their ocean homes. "I could never again listen happily to a thrush song," Carson wrote, "if I had not done all I could." She chose to go ahead with the book and to help protect the natural world in spite of her family duties and poor health.

"If I didn't at least try," she said, "I could never again be happy in nature."

By 1958, Carson was once more poring over scientific reports and writing letters to experts, as she gathered the research for her new book. Then, in December, her mother died. For Rachel Carson, overcome with grief, work on the new project became impossible. It did not comfort her to think that her mother had lived a long, full life.

From childhood, Rachel had found her mother to be a loving friend and constant teacher. For 50 years they had been companions, sharing their lives, adventures by the sea, and the success of Rachel's writing career. It was her mother who typed Rachel's final manuscripts. Maria Carson was the most important person in her daughter's life, and Rachel mourned for months.

At last, the memory of her mother helped Rachel Carson to start working on the book again. She could not forget Maria Carson's "love of life and of all living things." Nor could she forget how strongly her mother felt about this new project.

Carson imagined how pleased her mother would have been to see this book published. "She could fight fiercely against anything she believed wrong," Rachel wrote to a friend about her mother. "Knowing how she felt about that will help me return to it soon, and to carry it through to completion."

Rachel Carson did return to her research and writing. She grew determined that nothing else would prevent her from finishing this important task. She kept on working even after learning in 1960 that she had cancer. Medical treatment meant surgery and radiation therapy—and still, the doctors said, they might not be able to stop the spread of the disease.

Her sickness made progress on the book slow and difficult. But "more than ever," Rachel Carson wrote, "I am eager to get the book done."

Despite these setbacks, Carson finished her book. It was published in 1962. Called *Silent Spring*, it changed forever the way people thought about their world.

Silent Spring begins with a fable about an American town where people enjoyed the songs of birds in spring and caught fish from clear rivers and lakes. It was a place where wildflowers grew along the roadsides. There, "foxes barked in the hills and deer silently crossed the fields, half hidden in the mists of the fall morning."

Then, as if under some "evil spell," farm animals sickened and died. The birds were gone, the spring strangely silent. Brown, withered plants lined the roads, "as though swept by fire." And no one visited the rivers and lakes, "for all the fish had died."

"Everywhere was a shadow of death," Carson wrote.

No real town had suffered all of these misfortunes, Carson noted. But each one had happened somewhere. "What has already silenced the voices of spring in countless towns in America?" she asked. Her book gave the startling answer: chemicals used to kill insects and weeds.

Silent Spring describes how pesticides travel through the water supply, how they remain in the soil, and how they reach all levels of the food chain—insects, fish, birds, and mammals. Carson's book shows how "the history of life on earth has been a history of interaction between living things and their environment."

Now people have the power, she claimed, to change the very nature of their world. People have the power to upset the careful balance of the natural order, to pollute the air, earth, rivers, and seas with dangerous and even deadly materials. Carson called this pollution "a chain of evil." She warned that once the chain is started, it may be impossible to stop or reverse the effects of this damage to the earth.

Among the most dangerous of these pollutants are the chemical pesticides. "Chemicals sprayed on croplands or forests or gardens," Carson observed, "lie long in the soil, entering into living organisms, passing from one to another in a chain of poisoning and death."

"Can anyone believe," she asked, "it is possible to lay down such a barrage of poisons on the surface of the earth without making it unfit for all life?"

Chapter 6

The Closing Journey

Even before it reached the shelves of bookstores, *Silent Spring* came under attack. To the companies that earned millions of dollars making and selling pesticides, Rachel Carson's book was a threat.

Some people in the pesticide industry tried to scare Rachel Carson's readers. They insisted that if everyone followed her advice and stopped using pesticides, insects would overrun the world and swallow up the food supply. As a result, people would starve.

But Carson had never called for a complete ban on pesticides. Instead, she wrote in *Silent Spring* that these chemicals had to be used carefully by men and women who understood their dangers. At the same time, people needed to find safer ways to control insects.

The pesticide companies attacked more than Rachel Carson's book. They attacked the author herself. They said that she didn't have the facts. They said that Carson was emotional and unfair. Some people even suggested that *Silent Spring* was part of a plot to destroy America!

Luckily, not everyone listened to the critics of *Silent Spring*. Thousands of people read the book and formed their own opinions of what Rachel Carson had to say. Many readers wrote to thank Carson for her book. They

now understood the need to protect the environment from pollution. Some shared their own stories about pesticide poisoning or other forms of chemical pollution.

One well-known person who read *Silent Spring* was President John F. Kennedy. Troubled by the events that Carson depicted, the president asked his Science Advisory Committee to study pesticide use in the United States. After a careful investigation, this committee found that Rachel Carson was indeed correct. Its report, issued in 1963, agreed that chemical pesticides, as they were being used, threatened all forms of life. The report led to new laws controlling pesticide use in the years ahead.

As a tribute to her work on *Silent Spring*, Rachel Carson received numerous awards. By this time, however, she had become too ill to attend most of the ceremonies in her honor. Her cancer was getting worse, and in 1963 she suffered a heart attack. Although Carson recovered, she often needed to be in a wheelchair.

Despite her illnesses, Carson traveled to California as a guest of the Sierra Club, a conservation group. For years she had dreamed of seeing California's giant sequoia trees, and Carson knew that this trip would be her only chance. Then, in the summer of 1963, Rachel and Roger made their last visit together to Maine.

One morning in Maine, as the summer reached its end, Carson went outdoors with her friend and neighbor, Dorothy Freeman. Together, they watched a group of monarch butterflies flying south, as they do at that time of year. Both women knew that the lives of these beautiful creatures were almost over. "This was the closing journey of their lives," Rachel Carson wrote.

Like the butterflies, Carson was nearing the end of her life. As she watched, she realized that death was a part of nature's order. It brought her comfort to know that all living things complete the cycle of birth, growth, and death.

"When any living thing has come to the end of its cycle, we accept that end as natural," Carson wrote to Dorothy Freeman later that same day. "That is what these brightly fluttering bits of life taught me this morning. I found a deep happiness in it—so, I hope, may you. Thank you for this morning."

The lesson of that morning helped Carson prepare for her own death. It occurred on April 14, 1964, at her home in Silver Spring.

Chapter 7

A Fateful Power

"We have much to accomplish," Rachel Carson wrote in the 1940s, if future generations are to enjoy "a land as richly endowed in natural resources as the one we live in." That statement is just as true today.

Since Carson wrote *Silent Spring*, the federal government has banned the use of DDT and other pesticides known to be poisonous to humans. The government also checks the amount of pesticides in food to be sure it is within safe limits. Concerned farmers in every state are using smaller amounts of pesticides, and many now use natural methods of pest control.

The careless and unsafe use of pesticides still poses a risk to the natural environment and to human health. But as Rachel Carson understood, the problem of pesticides is just one part of a greater concern. Through science and technology, people have gained, in her words, "a fateful power to alter and destroy nature." Many people thought they could use this power to control the environment. But Rachel Carson urged her fellow human beings to control their own attitudes and actions instead. She asked people to work for "mastery, not of nature, but of ourselves."

In her quiet, careful way, Rachel Carson educated the world about the danger of pesticide use. As a tribute to her hard work and courage, the U.S. government created the Rachel Carson National Wildlife Refuge on the coast of Maine to protect the living things that she loved. But the greatest tribute to her life is the work of so many people today on behalf of the environment.

Rachel Carson's books continue to introduce millions of people to the life of the sea and shore. Nearly 30 years after her death, her words still bring the beauty and the harmony of the natural world to life.

"It is good to know that I shall live on even in the minds of many who do not know me," she wrote. It would please Rachel Carson to know that when people remember her, they think of "things that are beautiful and lovely."

Glossary

bathysphere   a round, metallic chamber that undersea divers use to descend to great depths

biology   the study of living things

conservation   the process by which natural resources are saved, or conserved

DDT   a chemical pesticide (abbreviation for dichloro-diphenyl-trichloroethane)

ecologist   a person who studies the relationship between living things and their environment

ecology   the study of living things in their environment

ecosystem   the network of relationships among living things and their environment

endangered species   a species that has so few members that it is in danger of dying out, or becoming extinct

environment   the physical world that surrounds a plant or animal

extinct   no longer in existence; describes a species of plant or animal that has died out

food chain   a series of plants and animals linked in a network of food relationships

habitat	the physical surroundings where a living thing makes its home
marine zoology	the study of sea and ocean animals
natural pest control	the use of natural methods, such as other living things, to control insect pests
oceanography	the study of the ocean
organism	a living thing
pesticide	a substance, often a strong chemical, used to kill insect pests
plankton	tiny plants and animals that float near the surface of a body of water
pollution	the process by which a natural environment is made unclean and unfit for living things
preservation	the process by which an environment is kept, or preserved, in its natural condition
species	a group of similar plants or animals that can produce offspring
wilderness area	an area of land or water permanently protected from development
wildlife	animals or plants living in a natural state
wildlife refuge	an area of land or water set aside as a protected home for wildlife

Index